AN HONEST DAY'S WORK:

Motivating Employees to Give Their Best

Twyla Dell

CRISP PUBLICATIONS, INC.
Los Altos, California

D1275501

AN HONEST DAY'S WORK

Motivating Employees to Give Their Best

CREDITS
Editor: **Michael G. Crisp**
Designer: **Carol Harris**
Typesetting: **Interface Studio**
Cover Design: **Carol Harris**
Artwork: **Ralph Mapson**

Copyright © 1988 by Crisp Publications, Inc.
Printed in the United States of America

Crisp books are distributed in Canada by Reid Publishing, Ltd., P.O. Box 7267, Oakville, Ontario, Canada L6J 6L6.

In Australia by Career Builders, P.O. Box 1051 Springwood, Brisbane, Queensland, Australia 4127.

And in New Zealand by Career Builders, P.O. Box 571, Manurewa, New Zealand.

Library of Congress Catalog Card Number 87-72484
Dell, Twyla
An Honest Day's Work
ISBN 0-931961-39-4

To Carl Blomgren for his patience and invaluable support.

ABOUT THIS BOOK

AN HONEST DAY'S WORK is not like most books. It has a unique "self-paced" format that encourages a reader to become personally involved. Designed to be "read with a pencil," there are an abundance of exercises, activities, assessments and cases that invite participation.

The objective of AN HONEST DAY'S WORK is to provide guidelines which will create working conditions that bring out the best in employees.

This book (and the other self-improvement titles listed on page 73) can be used effectively in a number of ways. Here are some possibilities:

—**Individual Study.** Because the book is self-instructional, all that is needed is a quiet place, some time, and a pencil. By completing the activities and exercises, a reader should not only receive valuable feedback, but also practical steps for self-improvement.

—**Workshops and Seminars.** This book is ideal for assigned reading prior to a workshop or seminar. With the basics in hand, the quality of the participation will improve, and more time can be spent on concept extensions and applications during the program. The book is also effective when it is distributed at the beginning of a session, and participants "work through" the contents.

—**Remote Location Training.** Books can be sent to those not able to attend "home office" training sessions.

There are other possibilities that depend on the objectives, program or ideas of the user.

One thing for sure, even after it has been read, this book will be looked at—and thought about—again and again.

TO THE READER

If you've ever been responsible for getting others to work hard, you know how frustrating that effort can be. Yet motivating others to give their best for an organization is the heart of management.

The heart of motivation is to give people what they *really* want from work. The more you are able to provide what they want, the more you should expect what you really want, namely, productivity, quality and service.

This book will explain what people want most in their jobs. It will also tell how to create an environment that will bring out the best in your employees. The heart of this book combines five levels of employee needs with the 10 qualities people want most in a job. This creates a simple, step-by-step plan for any manager or supervisor to follow.

Unlike other management books, AN HONEST DAY'S WORK deals with the heart of motivation—employee feelings that need to be recognized and handled. As a manager you deal with people's basic needs. This is where real motivation starts and ends. To motivate people to give their best, you, the manager must supply their needs. This book will help you do just that.

Tully Weiss

A ONE-PAGE PRODUCTIVITY PLAN...

This book contains a **one-page productivity plan** designed to get the best from the people who work for you. It is simple and it works the moment you put it into practice.

This is also a **one-idea-per-page book**. One idea on each page means you don't have to search for answers. You don't have to study. Just look at the heading for answers to the situation you are facing. The answers are here, ready to use. You do, though, need to keep a pencil handy as you turn the pages. You'll want to fill in the blanks to make this book **suitable for your needs** right now.

Five steps are presented that will help you get the best from your people. Each step has a **Bonus Section** with special advice. Each also has a story of real people who are getting the best from their workers. Good luck as you begin your journey.

TABLE OF CONTENTS

INTRODUCTION

In spite of better wages and working conditions than most countries, American workers often suffer from low morale and productivity. This gap between an employee's actual and potential output might be called the ''Commitment Gap.'' Managers approach the challenge of closing the Commitment Gap from many directions, but often with frustrating results.

Surveys have shown that American workers want to do their best but feel that management and ''the system'' keep them from it. Managers often create with the best of intentions the very conditions that lead to poor morale and low productivity.

In this section you will be able to analyze the Commitment Gap, become aware of the reasons behind it, and draw some conclusions about the productivity level of your staff.

SECTION I

CLOSE THE COMMITMENT GAP!

As we move from the Industrial to the Information Age, the quality of service we offer becomes increasingly important. We need both high quality product as well as the best possible service to remain competitive as an organization.

Service is given *to* people *by* people. To give excellent service, it is essential that people feel good about themselves and their jobs.

When service is given a high value, we change our focus from working with our hands to working with our hearts. We look for ways to give the best service possible, often beyond the customer's expectations. We look for ways to give a feeling of respect and value to each individual we serve.

To prosper and excel in the Information Age, organizations need to do the same for their employees. When the same measure of respect and value is given to employees, the organization wins! Employees will give little of what they do not personally experience.

Therefore, to excel in the Information Age, develop the human potential of your people.

SOME STATISTICS

At a time when we need to pull together as a team, work hard to hold market share, create and introduce new products and increase profits, we seem to be slipping. Workers often look and act as though they are deliberately slowing down work, just getting by, putting forth no great effort, stealing time and avoiding important tasks.

What is wrong with today's workers? A recent poll[1] showed that:

- 88% want to "work hard and do their best on the job."

- 55% said they had an "inner need to do their very best regardless of pay."

BUT—

- 50% said they "worked just hard enough to avoid getting fired."

AND—

- 75% said they "could be *significantly* more effective on the job."

When asked why they didn't work harder, employees said:

- "Our bosses don't know how to make us work harder."

- "We don't get paid to work harder."

Does this sound familiar? Do those answers bother you?

---

[1]From a 1980 Gallup poll as quoted in RE-INVENTING THE CORPORATION by John Naisbitt, Warner Books, 1985, page 85.

MEET THE DIFFICULT EMPLOYEE

Fortunately, difficult employees are a minority in the workplace. Still, even a few can foster unhappiness and unrest. How do employees become ''difficult?''

Most employees don't start out that way. Most want to work hard. They want to fill their needs through work, to be secure, to belong, to win recognition, to have fun and learn new skills.

But often what workers want from work is not what employers give them. Employers want a product or service produced with as little hassle and as much profit as possible. Since they are product or profit motivated, they sometimes pay too little attention to the real needs of their employees.

Without realizing what they are doing, managers can create the kind of negative atmosphere that causes employees to become difficult.

When there is a ''them against us'' atmosphere or when products, services, deadlines or profits are valued higher than an individual's potential and feelings, difficult employees will multiply. They come out of hiding when their basic human needs are not met.

People have long been considered expenses, while stock, supplies, buildings and inventory are viewed on the balance sheet as assets. Smart employers are now beginning to realize that people are the assets. The other things are less important to the success of the organization.

WHEN DIFFICULT EMPLOYEES ACT UP

Difficult employees are those who swim against the current. They are the ones who "act out" their unhappiness by complaining, goofing off, stealing time and sometimes being destructive. They are often bright, creative people who find they can't express themselves the way they'd like to on the job.

Have you worked with people who:

☐ Want to think for themselves rather than be told what to do?

☐ Have ideas on how to organize and run things better?

☐ Get bored with repetitious work?

☐ Become unproductive when not challenged?

☐ Dislike working for disorganized managers?

☐ Are unhappy working at something when they don't see the final product?

☐ Come in late, leave early?

☐ Hate being left out of meetings they can contribute to?

☐ Want someone to listen when they have suggestions on how to do things better?

☐ Resent working with poor tools and equipment?

☐ Are not content to work without the big picture?

☐ Want to have a say in how things turn out?

☐ Insist on variety of pace and tasks?

☐ Beg for more responsibility and authority?

☐ Want to break off and have some fun—maybe even outside the office?

☐ Push to learn new skills?

☐ Want to be recognized when they do good work?

☐ Hate it when you don't remember their names?

As you checked off the boxes, did you recognize any of your own behaviors as either an employee or manager?

WHY EMPLOYEES DON'T GET THE JOB DONE!

Usually, there are three reasons people don't get the job done. Regardless of what reasons people may give, the answer may be one of these three:

1. They don't know how.

2. Something or someone keeps them from it.

3. They don't want to...

CHECK THESE OUT!

Of the three possibilities described on the previous page what could you do to improve productivity in your area? List specific actions below:

They don't know how.

Do any of your employees need training? Who could benefit from training? (Be specific.)

Name   Training Needed

_____

_____

_____

_____

Something or someone keeps them from it.

Are there obstacles in your area?

_____

_____

_____

_____

They don't want to.

Do you know why not?

Name   Why?

_____

_____

_____

_____

ENTER TIME THEFT

What happens when people don't know how to do their jobs, can't do their jobs because something is keeping them from it, or don't want to do their jobs? The answer is that they don't work to their potential. Instead they commit ''time crime.''

Call it what you like, it is the disappearance of time at the organization's expense. Whether workers slow the work pace, avoid carrying out tasks, look for another job on company time, make social phone calls or any other activity that robs the company of needed results, it is *time theft*.

Not much has been written about time theft but it is a costly problem—millions of productive hours are lost each year. Time theft haunts every manager.

How many kinds of time theft have you observed? Check them off below.

☐ Work flow is held up by other departments.

☐ Work flow within a department is held up.

☐ Too many/few employees for amount of work.

☐ Low morale slows work.

☐ Negative attitude toward _____ slows down work.

☐ Non job-related activities such as _____ take time.

☐ Laziness or procrastination created by _____ .

☐ Inefficient management

☐ Other _____

☐ Other _____

CLOSE THE COMMITMENT GAP!

If you could have highly motivated workers who work to their fullest potential while producing excellent quality and product, would you want that? Of course! This kind of work is called "commitment." Commitment of employees to the organization's vision and values, to excellence and productivity is every manager's dream.

The first step in achieving this happy state is to analyze and close "the Commitment Gap." The Commitment Gap is the difference between the time people are paid for working and the amount of time actually spent in productive labor.

Percent of time worked*									
10	20	30	40	50	60	70	80	90	100

Circle the average amount of time you think those around you work in productive ways. Is there a gap between what you circled and 100%? If so, you need to find ways to improve productivity.

MEASURE YOUR PRODUCTIVITY

---

*(Don't confuse looking busy with productivity, creative avoidance with output, slowdown with potential output or sabotage with problem solving.)

MEASURE THE PRODUCTIVITY

What would be the *IMPROVEMENT IN PRODUCTIVITY* to you and your organization if you could close the Commitment Gap? How many hours more of productive labor could you create?

INVESTMENT:

Number of employees × number of hours paid:

RETURN:

Number of employees × number of hours productively worked:

> **THE DIFFERENCE BETWEEN THE INVESTMENT AND THE RETURN IS THE COST TO YOUR ORGANIZATION.**

Is there untapped potential in your department?

OPEN TO GROWTH

It is acknowledged that workers in the future will require more mental skills. Managing creative people demands more sensitivity. As people become better informed, they expect to be treated better at work.

Treating employees better means finding ways to get them excited about their jobs. When ways are implemented to do that, it will help close the Commitment Gap. It isn't always easy to close the Commitment Gap, but it is possible. And the payoff is well worth the effort. Liberating an employee's potential is like finding gold. You may have to dig for it, but it brings great rewards when discovered.

When employee satisfaction improves the Commitment Gap begins to close. The atmosphere of the organization changes. Expectations become positive. The pace quickens, people act with vigor and purpose. Morale rises.

The following pages will provide some thoughts about how to close the Commitment Gap in your organization.

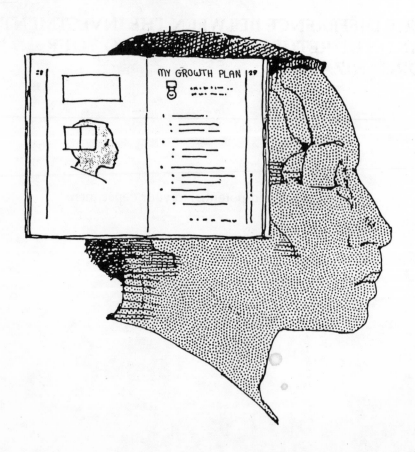

WHAT MAKES EMPLOYEES HAPPY?

Every worker wants to feel good about doing his or her job. That's called ''employee satisfaction.'' Employee satisfaction is made up of several factors, but they can be related to *five levels of need* first described by a psychologist in the 1960's, Abraham Maslow. Maslow said that each person has the same needs and that we all spend each day satisfying one or more of those needs.

We need to survive.

Our most basic need is **to survive**. You might compare that to a cave man killing a rabbit and crawling into a cave to cook and eat it.

We need security.

The next need is **security**. The cave man may kill several rabbits, then roll a stone in front of the cave door to protect his assets.

We need to belong.

Soon the cave man may feel lonely. Since he has enough rabbit for today and tomorrow, he invites some other cave people he enjoys to share with him. He has now satisfied the need for **belonging**.

We need prestige.

Once he has others around, he appoints himself chief. This satisfies his need for **prestige**.

We need self-fulfillment.

Finally, his group is secure enough to decorate the cave walls with paintings and dance and sing. He is praised for having made it all possible and has reached the level of **self-fulfillment**.

WHERE ARE YOU ON THE LADDER?

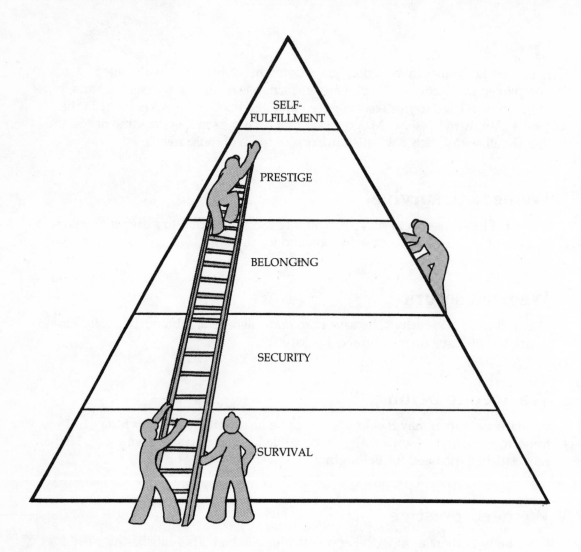

Maslow's Hierarchy shows that all humans have the same basic needs. How do these needs get satisfied in the average job? Put an "X" on the level where you think you spend most of your time. Are you at the survival level or closer to self-fulfillment? Or do you (like most people) operate mostly in the security or prestige levels?

Look again at the triangle. Circle your "X" and then place new "Xs" with the initials of others you work with, and where you think they fit.

TEN QUALITIES EMPLOYEES WANT IN A JOB

Most organizations today are moving away from making people fit the job and moving toward making the job fit people. Jobs are becoming more flexible. Workplaces are becoming more responsive to workers' needs.

To attract and keep good people it will become increasingly necessary to create an atmosphere of learning and growth. This calls for a new kind of supervisor— one who can:

■ coach
■ teach
■ lead employees to new challenges
■ make people feel good about themselves
■ keep individuals motivated and interested.

Following are the ten qualities that people want most from their jobs as reported by the Public Agenda Foundation, 1983:

1. To work for efficient managers

2. To think for themselves

3. To see the end result of their work

4. To be assigned interesting work

5. To be informed

6. To be listened to

7. To be respected

8. To be recognized for their efforts

9. To be challenged

10. To have opportunities for increased skill development.

ARE YOU RECEIVING THE TOP TEN?

How many of the ten qualities have you been *getting* in your job? To effectively supervise others, it helps if you are receiving what you need to give.

In the following exercise, rate yourself with a 3 if you are satisfied with what you are *getting*. Rate yourself a 1 if the supply is scarce, and a 0 if you're not receiving any.

_____ I work for an efficient manager.

_____ I am encouraged to think for myself.

_____ I see the end result of my work.

_____ I have interesting work.

_____ I am listened to when I have ideas on how to do things better.

_____ I am informed about what is going on.

_____ I receive respect for my efforts.

_____ I am recognized for a job well done.

_____ I am challenged by what I do.

_____ I get opportunities for skill development.

_____ SCORE:

A score of 24 or more means you're at the top of your ladder. A score of 15 to 23—suggests you're doing OK and can make some positive changes. A score of 8-14 indicates trouble. You may be a wage slave or simply filling time. Put out your resume. 0-7 means you're falling off the ladder and need to seriously assess your career choice.

ARE YOU GIVING THE TOP TEN?

It's equally important to know how *to give* the top ten qualities. It's easier to give them, if you're receiving them. Even if that's not true, however, to get the most from your people and make your workplace the best it can be, you need to concentrate on giving as many of these qualities as possible.

Rate yourself again, this time on how much you're *giving*. Score a 3 for high, 2 for average, 1 for below average, 0 for not at all.

_____ I am an efficient manager.

_____ I encourage and teach employees to think for themselves.

_____ I arrange work so employees can see the end result.

_____ I divide work to make it as interesting as possible to everyone.

_____ I listen when there are ideas on how to do things better.

_____ I inform those who need to know about what is going on.

_____ I treat employees like professionals at all times.

_____ I recognize individuals for good work both formally and informally.

_____ I offer challenges whenever possible.

_____ I encourage skill development.

_____ SCORE

How did you score? 24-30 means you're an outstanding supervisor. 15-23 means you have the potential to be a leader. Keep practicing. 8-14 says you're getting the picture but your workers are enduring in hopes of better days. 0-7 move aside and let someone else take over.

STEPS TO IMPROVED PRODUCTIVITY

It is interesting to note that the ten qualities employees want in a job described on page 13 match nicely with Maslow's five levels of need described on page 11. A manager sensitive to both Maslow's needs and the ten qualities employees want in a job, is on the road to success. Some qualities fit several levels. For purposes of this book, we have assigned qualities as shown below. The important thing is to learn how to deliver each quality effectively.

► *The basic human need is* **survival**. The core of employee satisfaction is to:

1. Work for an efficient manager
2. Think for self

► The next level of need is **security**. At this level employees need to:

3. See the end result of their work
4. Be involved in interesting work

► The third level of need is **belonging**. For belonging, employees need to:

5. Be listened to
6. Be informed

► The fourth level is **prestige**. For prestige, employees need:

7. Respect
8. Recognition

► The final level of need is **self-fulfillment**. At this level, employees need:

9. A challenge
10. Skill development

YOUR ONE-PAGE PRODUCTIVITY PLAN

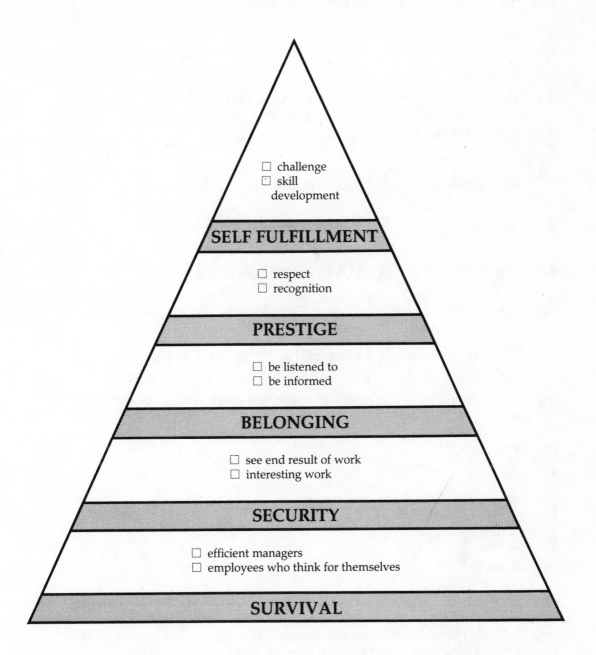

☐ challenge
☐ skill development

SELF FULFILLMENT

☐ respect
☐ recognition

PRESTIGE

☐ be listened to
☐ be informed

BELONGING

☐ see end result of work
☐ interesting work

SECURITY

☐ efficient managers
☐ employees who think for themselves

SURVIVAL

Start at the bottom and work your way up to become a ''top'' manager.

SECTION II

FIVE STEPS TO SUCCESS

A journey toward a productive, happy workplace begins with the first step. This section of AN HONEST DAY'S WORK guides you through five steps which spell the acronym "LEARN."

The First Step is   **L** earn to Lead

The Second Step is   **E** xamine Expectations

The Third Step is   **A** ct Like You Care

The Fourth Step is   **R** espect Employees as Professionals

The Fifth Step is   **N** ever Stifle Personal Growth

Together the five steps will lead any manager to a more productive and happy workplace.

The "L" stands for "Learn to Lead." That means becoming an efficient and effective time and work organizer so that you don't stand in the way of your own organization's productivity. That kind of organized approach creates time and space for you to be with your people when you need to be and to give yourself room to grow. It's difficult to move up the ladder or try for new goals when your daily work is in disarray.

STEP 1: | **LEARN TO LEAD**

The first skill is to show *you can lead*. Do this two ways by *being efficient* and *teaching employees to think for themselves*. A manager who is disorganized and inefficient lowers the standard of excellence and creates a state of mediocrity.

Employees respect excellence. They want their leaders to be efficient and top-of-the-line in everything they do.

What does efficient mean? It means more than just being neat. It means:

☐ being competent
   ☐ skillful
      ☐ capable
         ☐ and productive.

BE EFFICIENT ⟹

It also means *not* being:

         ☐ ignorant of the job needs
      ☐ unskilled in getting results
    ☐ unable to handle new situations
  ☐ lazy, inconsistent and inattentive.

Efficiency not only *saves* time, it *makes* time to satisfy the other levels of employee satisfaction.

THE EFFICIENT-MANAGER CHECKLIST

Rate yourself for efficiency. Give yourself a 3 for statements you feel totally describe your situation, 2 for those that are somewhat true, 1 for any that are not very true of what you do and 0 if the statement does not describe you at all.

_____ 1. I know the technical aspects of my job thoroughly.

_____ 2. I have organized the work flow very efficiently.

_____ 3. I control the work flow to match the way it was organized.

_____ 4. I know enough about the big picture to relate what I'm doing to others who need to know.

_____ 5. I am personally productive.

_____ 6. I have developed tracking systems to monitor results.

_____ 7. I am neat and efficient in my work area as an example to others.

_____ 8. I can handle new situations easily when they arise.

_____ 9. I'm skillful at combining tasks for greater efficiency.

_____ 10. I encourage subordinates to suggest ideas for efficiency.

_____ 11. I am constantly on the lookout for ways to do things better.

_____ 12. I help my manager be more efficient by anticipating needs and being prepared.

_____ SCORE

If you scored 28-36, congratulate yourself, you're in orbit. 19-27 Hurray! You're leaving the launch pad. 11-18 You're learning but not ready to fly. Below 11, back to ''ground school'' to learn the secrets of flight.

EMPLOYEES WHO THINK FOR THEMSELVES

Those who think for themselves do not suffer from *analysis paralysis, boredom or mental malnutrition*. Train your employees to make decisions that work for them, for you, for the customer and for the organization.

The basis of getting workers to think for themselves is to encourage them to ask questions, to listen and then offer guidance. Over time, they will learn to ask questions in order to discover answers that will serve the best interests of everyone involved.

Following are some sample questions which will help an employee check for understanding:

1. What has to happen for this to work?

2. And then what? By when?

3. What would happen if we didn't do this?

4. Is that the result we want?

5. If not, what *is* the result we want?

6. What do we have to do to get it?

7. How does this help reach our goal, your goal?

Add your own:

8. _____

9. _____

10. _____

A manager can't think for everyone. The basis of survival is to teach others to think for themselves.

BONUS SECTION: *Pass on the Vision*

What is a "vision?" It is a word picture describing a scene, circumstance or event. In historic times only prophets and soothsayers had visions. Today everyone needs one. Visions are roadmaps for the mind. They are the mark, the target toward which everything travels.

Without vision a person must depend on others for guidance. Without such guidance it is easy to wander in the dark. Organizations are the same way. Without a vision of where they are going, they can flounder.

It is essential for each organization from top to bottom to have a vision of where it is headed and how to get there. The organization's vision is the goal—what it is working toward becoming. Visions are sometimes called "mission statements." It is the responsibility of each manager to lead others toward the vision of the organization. Every department in every company needs to be in the process of becoming better, more efficient and more effective at what it does.

A vision, then, is a description of your mission when it is accomplished. Your job as leader is to help others

■ *see it!*

■ *want it!*

■ *reach it!*

SHARE THE VISION!

Why?

Why would it be important for you as a manager of people to share with your fellow workers the vision toward which you're striving? Wouldn't it be easier just to tell them what to do and correct them when they miss? That used to be the way management worked. But with better informed workers who demand more participation in planning and carrying out tasks, they want to know where they're going. Why share the vision? *Because, your employees can help you get there!*

How?

How do you share what you're trying to accomplish with others in your organization? You can do it a number of different ways:

Large groups	Small groups
memos	meetings
video announcements	on-the-spot guidance
training films	goal setting sessions
posters	performance appraisals
speeches	one-on-one conversations
other publications	awards and incentives

Which have you used? Which have worked? Which haven't? Why?

CREATING THE VISION

An organization's vision can be broken into several parts. It should explain the values a company has about itself as a business, about its employees and about its customers. The vision further describes where the company or organization is going—(the target), and how it plans to get there.

THE ORGANIZATION

What are the values of the organization Will it be the finest, fastest, smallest, most-service oriented, most complete service, best quality or product, lowest priced, etc.?

THE CUSTOMER

Who is the customer and why is he or she special? How will you service the needs of the customer? Will you offer 24-hour turn around, complete curbside service, top-of-the-line, constant attention, self service, white glove treatment etc.?

THE EMPLOYEES

Who are your employees? What qualities do you expect from them? Professionals, experts, most qualified, best paid, drug-free, well-trained, most polite and cheerful, best technical training, etc.?

THE DIRECTION

Where do you want to be in five years? Biggest in the world, 10% market share, finest in the downtown, upscale from Neiman-Marcus, 100 units nationwide, Walmart, watch out! etc.

WHAT IS YOUR VISION?

As a leader, when you can accurately describe the vision of your organization, you have established a base of understanding that can be passed along to others. This makes your organization stronger when all members strive for a common goal.

Try describing some values below for your organization, your customers, your employees and your direction to reflect how well you understand your vision.

YOUR ORGANIZATION:

_____

_____

_____

YOUR CUSTOMERS:

_____

_____

_____

YOUR EMPLOYEES:

_____

_____

_____

YOUR DIRECTION:

_____

_____

Have you developed a true and complete picture of where your organization is going? Can you describe what is important to you, what you believe in and what you are trying to create?

CASE SITUATION #1

How do you turn a small, struggling branch of a large corporation into a thriving, productive, profitable enterprise? Brad was given that assignment when he took over a staff of eight in a troubled division of a major organization. Building the operation to a highly profitable unit with 250 employees took time and vision.

The eight employees initially didn't see themselves as part of a large, vital organization. Separated by 500 miles from the main office, they worked at their own pace. They viewed their jobs in relation to the local market. Their products were good, but not better than anything else in that region.

When Brad arrived, he changed that. He made the goal of the parent company clear to each person. Brad now says, "Everyone in this organization knows our goals. We expect to be the best at what we do compared to anyone in the country." He broke his operation's goals into three areas:

1) A profitable rate of growth

2) Develop new customers and service existing ones in a superior way

3) Train employees to accept personal responsibility for productivity and profitability.

"Everything we do, every decision we make, we measure by those three points. And I do mean 'we.' All employees are involved in decisions that affect their productivity."

The next letter in "LEARN" is "E" for "Examine Expectations."

Too often it is an easy matter to hire people to fit a job that works well on paper but does not fit the human spirit.

The Industrial Age made great use of "human assembly lines." That philosophy has changed as people have become better informed about motivation. During this same period employee expectations of job satisfaction have also risen greatly.

This second step shows you how to provide security for employees by examining and matching your expectations of their jobs against theirs.

STEP 2: EXAMINE EXPECTATIONS

Two factors managers often overlook are that people like to see the end result of their efforts and they enjoy work when it is interesting. Amazingly, these two aspects are often undervalued.

Examine the expectations you have for your employees. Do you expect them to put out a high level of productivity if they don't feel involved in the end result? Are they bored doing the same task over and over and over? Do you accept that boredom as a primary ingredient of their job? Do you feel that allowing them to see the final outcome is unimportant?

When workers don't see the end result of their activities, it is hard for them to get excited about what they do. It is hard for them to feel any ownership in their work. In fact, the smaller the role a worker has on a given project, without positive feedback, the less that person feels like improving his or her output.

When you involve workers and explain their responsibility as it relates to the end product or service, then they know what to expect. Knowing what to expect gives most people a desire to contribute. Not knowing makes too many of them non-caring and ineffective—feelings that create low productivity.

REORGANIZE THE WORK FLOW

Sometimes, simply rearranging the flow of work will boost productivity. Studies have shown that almost any attention paid to the flow of work will have a positive effect.

One successful manager moves equipment and work stations and reorganizes duties regularly. She is willing to experiment to achieve greater efficiency. The employees help her engage in planning the moving of equipment.

The key point here is that the employees are involved in the decision-making process. Questions such as ''what would work better?,'' ''how can we get more out of this situation?'' ''how do we reduce the noise level?'' help the workers focus on improved productivity and come up with their own solutions.

One assembly line worker worked for 17 years doing the same repetitive task. When the work flow was rearranged to give him total responsibility for customer contact, problem solving and followup, his productivity went up **40%**.

Take a close look at the work flow arrangement in your area of responsibility. What could be done to change it for the better? Ask some questions of your employees. Get them involved with answers and plans.

MAKE WORK INTERESTING

MAKE WORK INTERESTING

The second need at this level of employee satisfaction is to make work *interesting*. Workers who do primarily only one thing all day, every day, quickly become bored.

To guard against boredom there are several things you might consider. These include rewriting job descriptions, rearranging work flows, giving more responsibility for problem solving, providing recognition for a job well done, etc. Loosen up and liberate the potential of the people working for you and you will be rewarded with improved morale and higher productivity.

Check yourself with these questions:

_____ I regularly discuss decisions with my employees.

_____ Employees are comfortable giving me their opinions and advice.

_____ I listen to employee comments, consider them and provide feedback.

_____ We often make group decisions.

_____ I make sure my employees feel involved with the end product.

_____ I make sure they understand the vision toward which we are working.

_____ I give employees authority to make meaningful decisions.

_____ I hold employees responsible for their decisions.

_____ We have developed a system in which we all profit from good decisions.

_____ I constantly check to see that pace, variety and involvement in work is designed to maintain high interest.

_____ SCORE

> Give yourself a 3 for always, 2 for sometimes, 1 for once in a while, 0 for never. If you scored between 23-30 you've taken the lid off your people's potential. At 16-22 your people are ready to grow. If between 9-15 paralysis is taking over. Below 9 you have created some zombies.

The next page provides a guide to problem solving. Problem solving not only makes work interesting, it helps workers see the result of their efforts. Ownership of problem solving pays off. Interest runs high, enthusiasm increases, morale goes up. People feel they help control the outcome.

Bonus Section: *S.O.S.: Solution Finder*

Situation + *Opportunity* = *Solution*

Here's the Situation: Your staff is very busy. They're working at full steam every day. Each Monday morning you conduct a staff meeting. During meetings people are needed to answer phones and attend to other details. To miss these meetings is to not know what's going on. No one has been taking minutes. Since some of the material is confidential, it can't just be posted. There has been no way established to get good information from the staff meeting to those who can't attend.

Here's the Opportunity: Now that we've described in detail, it's time to look at the opportunity. We can redesign the communication flow through new responsibilities, new work flow, new scheduling and increase team spirit at the same time.

Here's the Solution: Brainstorm among your staff for as many different solutions as possible. *Put down a minimum of 20 ideas.* This will force the group past some obvious answers into something more creative. Then assign responsibility and deadlines for putting the plan into action. Use the form on the next page to organize thoughts. By the way, how would you solve this situation?

S.O.S. = SITUATION OPPORTUNITY SOLUTION

1. Situation: Describe the situation in *detail*.

2. Opportunity: State your goal in positive terms. Describe the outcome you would like to see achieved.

3. Solution: Brainstorm 20 possible approaches to achieving the goal. Then choose the best suggestions and organize into action steps.

Action step 1): _____ Date to initiate: _____

Action step 2): _____ Date to initiate: _____

Action step 3): _____ Date to initiate: _____

Action step 4): _____ Date to initiate _____

Responsibility to coordinate:

_____

Deadline for completion:

_____

CASE SITUATION #2

Morale and productivity were low when Shelley took over as administrator of a county office. The office had received bad publicity from the local newspaper for a situation that had lacked foresight and effective follow through. Her employees were defensive and bored.

Shelley decided to change the atmosphere by reorganizing the work flow among her staff. Some had not done any different tasks in years. She asked them to help her design new information systems. They did. She made sure they got out of the office to see the end results of decisions.

Shelley then met with the editor of the paper and showed him that bad publicity was really counter productive to both their needs. He toured the office and asked many questions to understand the situation. He arranged for a more positive story about changes that had been made since the critical articles appeared.

When some of the employees were recognized in the newspaper for good work, she wrote that person a note of congratulations. A once dead office began to thrive again.

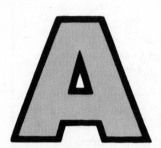

The next letter in "LEARN" is "A" for "Act Like You Care."

When employees feel they come first with their manager, customers will feel they come first with the employees. It's much easier to give when you are receiving. As managers listen, respond, and care for their employees, the employees do a better job of caring for customers. Managers' behavior becomes reinforced in a self-perpetuating cycle.

STEP 3: ACT LIKE YOU CARE

To get people to feel they belong, there is no better way to show an attitude of caring than by getting them involved and then listening to their comments.

Show you care by *listening*. Listening to employees *when they have ideas on how to do things better* is one of the most important things managers can do. Companies that listen normally get higher productivity and excellent two-way communication. They create the climate for bottom-up suggestions that get heard, used and appreciated.

When employees are not asked for their opinion, or worse, asked but not taken seriously, they become disconnected from the vision. They don't participate in the future of the organization the same way as others do. Being listened to is one of the most important ways people contribute to an organization. If that is denied, they lose interest and turn their energies to other things.

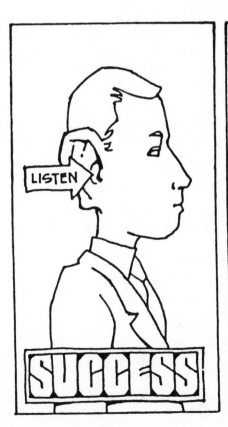

LEARN TO LISTEN*

Here are some guidelines for listening to employees:

■ *Treat them as professionals*—they'll be more likely to respond professionally if that is the attitude conveyed.

■ *Request the details as they see the situation*—take notes if necessary, but ask questions that give you as much information about their view as possible.

■ *Make no value judgements*—listen, nod and make notes and stay neutral until they have finished. Don't add opinions like "You know that won't work." Concentrate on the information in a friendly way.

■ *Reply as soon as possible*—people like to hear an answer—even a polite "that won't work in this situation because"—or at least a progress report of what is being done. Otherwise they feel left out, overlooked or unimportant—all feelings you want to avoid.

■ *Consider the "hidden" message*—there are sometimes other messages behind the information employees provide—a need for recognition, a desire to blame others, criticism of management, etc. Listen to what is not being said as well as what is being said.

■ *Provide follow-up opportunities*—Use the S.O.S. approach to create solutions.

---

*For an excellent book on listening, order *Effective Listening Skills* by Diane Bone from page 73.

KEEP EMPLOYEES INFORMED

The other side of the belonging level of satisfaction is to *keep your employees informed*. Without information they can't know what's going on. They won't know what progress is being made toward the organization's goals and won't know how to help make things happen.

It is natural to feel left out when information is lacking. Just as with being listened to, employees can feel unimportant, overlooked and undervalued if they do not receive regular feedback.

Often when employees don't get enough information or are not listened to, they form subgroups to manufacture their own information. These are called "grapevines," "cliques," or "rumor mills." Instead of spending time and energy helping to achieve the objectives of the organization, they create other diversions.

When employees in any subgroup are left out, the employer loses both productivity and commitment. The organization suffers.

FEELING LIKE YOU BELONG BY BEING LISTENED TO AND BEING INFORMED **IS ONE OF THE GREATEST WAYS TO CLOSE** *THE COMMITMENT GAP*.

A LISTENING AND INFORMING SURVEY

How important is "belonging" as a success factor to you? Take the self-test and find out:

Give yourself a 3 for absolutely, 2 for some of the time, 1 for once in a while and 0 for never.

Listening

> Be honest with yourself about your listening style. When employees discuss work items with you, how well do you listen?

_____ I know the value of listening for the morale of my employees.

_____ I listen to all members of my staff as one professional to another.

_____ I obtain the necessary details from each conversation.

_____ I give no value judgements while listening.

_____ I create time to listen.

_____ I know the value of listening to the success of my job.

_____ I reply as soon as possible when a reply is required.

_____ I coach others in listening skills.

_____ I listen for any hidden messages.

_____ I provide followup and an opportunity for solutions.

_____ I'm a great listener!

_____ Score   TOTAL _____

Informing

> How well do you inform your people? When employees want to know what's going on, what do you do?

_____ I know the value of keeping employees informed.

_____ I give equal information to everyone who needs to know.

_____ I prefer to inform employees in person rather than by memo.

_____ I create time to inform.

_____ I make it a point to update those who are absent.

_____ I informally share information to help others on a regular basis.

_____ I include all involved personnel when new developments occur.

_____ I withhold as little information as possible.

_____ I use information to help get everyone excited about the job.

Score _____

A score of 51-60 shows your ears and mind are open! 41-50 means you're doing a solid job. 31-40 means your people often feel left out. 21-30 suggests a real problem. Open your eyes, ears and mind.

Bonus Section: *Your Unique Style*

Belonging means feeling appreciated. One feeling an employee needs is an appreciation for any of his or her unique qualities. When this occurs, it increases a feeling of belonging. People who appreciate one another tend to view themselves as part of a team. They share ideas, values and goals.

For over 2,000 years, four basic personality types have been recognized. Hippocrates first described them in 400 B.C..Though the names have changed and information has been added to Hippocrates' original description, the four types have stayed basically the same. Although each of us tends to be more of one type than any other, we have some of all types in us.

Hippocrates named the personality types after various fluids in the body: "choleric" for hard-driving and impatient individuals, "sanguine" for happy-go-lucky types, "phlegmatic" for slow moving, steady souls, and "melancholy" for those of us who are sensitive and introspective.

Today the types are often called driver or dominant, inspirational or influencer, analytical or steady and compliant or amiable. Which type are you?

FOUR PERSONALITY TYPES

In each square below you will likely see yourself. But wait. Choose the square that is *most* like the real you!

THE PIONEER
(choleric)

Pusher, Producer, imPatient, Powerful, Persistent, exasPerating, to the Point, unPredictable, comPelling, Problem solver, OverstePs Prerogatives

WHEELER DEALER
(sanguine)

Debonaire, Dashing, Devilish, no Detail, Delightful, aDaptive, iDea person, Democratic, non-Dictatorial, Desiring to help and please, Diplomatic, Dynamic

CAPTAIN CAUTION
(phlegmatic)

Caretaker, Conservator, Keep the balance, Consistent, Kind, Careful, Calming influence, Cooperating, Concise, Conventional

SYSTEMS THINKER
(melancholy)

Sensitive, proceSSor, need Sensor, Stage manager, Synergist, Systematic, Supportive, Synthesizer, Self-critical, Standardized, Sympathetic

WHICH PERSONALITY TYPE ARE YOU?

Which type is most like you? _____

Which is your next strongest style? _____

Which is least like you? _____

For fun, see if you can list selected associates, employees, friends, etc. with their primary style.

Name	Most likely style
_____	_____
_____	_____
_____	_____
_____	_____
_____	_____
_____	_____
_____	_____

WHAT EACH PERSONALITY TYPE NEEDS TO BE EFFECTIVE

Regardless of personality type, each requires a different approach by a leader to get the best from that person. No two types should be treated the same. It is part of the leader's job to learn how to handle each personality type to get the best performance from everyone.

THE PIONEER NEEDS:

- lots of challenges
- correction when needed
- to be shown *what* you want
- some prestige
- an opportunity to learn new skills
- a feeling of competence

WHEELER DEALERS THRIVE ON:

- democratic guidance
- lots of people contact
- plenty of variety
- fun
- public recognition
- being told *who* is on the team

CAPTAIN CAUTION WANTS:

- a stable environment
- to be shown *how* to do
- an encouragement of analytical talent
- plenty of warning before change happens
- to be probed for real feelings
- economic security

SYSTEMS THINKERS LIKE TO:

- create harmony
- to be shown *why* it's done
- use a detail approach
- avoid criticism
- be given praise in private
- have time to process information

WHEN UNDER STRESS

Everyone responds differently to pressure. Each personality type acts a certain way when the going gets tough. Understanding this behavior will help a leader avoid problems. Following are some reactions common to each type. Realize that any individual may not show all of these.

THE PIONEER SAYS:

"I'm in charge here."

"I'm bored and restless."

"I don't care, I'm doin' it anyway."

"I can't stand routine."

"I'd just as soon work alone."

"To get it done quickly, I'll do it myself."

WHEELER DEALER SAYS:

"I want everyone to love me."

"I don't care, I'll give my heart."

"I've changed my mind today."

"I love you all; you're great"

"I don't have time for facts."

"Gee, where has the time gone?"

CAPTAIN CAUTION SAYS:

"Don't rock the boat!"

"I can't seem to get going."

"I like things just as they are."

"Tradition is good enough for me."

"I'm waiting for my orders."

"I don't care, I'm not changing."

SYSTEMS THINKER SAYS:

"It's not my decision."

"There's no rule about this."

"I'll have to look it up."

"I don't care, I didn't do it."

"Let's get more information first."

"I can't change til you tell why."

WHAT'S IN IT FOR YOU?

What is your payoff for recognizing and dealing with the different personality styles? Mainly, your life as a leader and manager will be much easier if you stop struggling with different styles and adapt to them instead. You can help your people be their best by giving them work that is most appropriate for their style.

When you encourage each one to be "their style":

THE PIONEER BECOMES:

- a risktaker
- a decision maker
- an independent worker
- a change agent
- results-oriented person

Other _____

_____

_____

WHEELER DEALERS TURN INTO:

- inspiring leaders
- diplomats
- enthusiastic workers
- favorable impression givers
- contributors of high morale

Other _____

_____

_____

CAPTAIN CAUTION CONTRIBUTES:

- steady work
- patient approach
- being a loyal employee
- following instructions
- being task oriented

Other _____

_____

_____

SYSTEMS THINKERS PROVIDE:

- specialized skills
- details
- high standards
- careful decisions
- a high level of accuracy

Other _____

_____

_____

HOW TO USE THE STYLES

Though we each have a dominant or "home" style, our challenge is to use the other styles when they are desirable. The more versatile you are, the greater your options will be.

As a manager or leader, you know that one thing you have to do is to push for results, plow new ground and explore different paths. This brings out the *PIONEER* in you. When you need to be a pioneer, become comfortable with those qualities and use them.

Once you've found the right path, you need to be more interested in people. These individuals need to be led using diplomacy and tact. Bring employees together to reach the goal you've mutually established. That's the time to be a *WHEELER DEALER*. Your ability to influence and inspire will help get the job done.

As you develop people to become productive, you need to develop some routines. You're still using your first two styles but now the organization and maintenance phase requires task-oriented skills. You have to watch expenses, work flow and morale. You become more like *CAPTAIN CAUTION* during this phase.

Now it's time to standardize the progress you have made. So you call upon your detail-oriented characteristics to make sure things are done right. You become analytical and control results as a *SYSTEMS THINKER*.

CASE SITUATION #3

Joe is supervisor of a large group of retail clerks. From experience he has observed that each person has a unique style. Joe has learned that it is easier to capitalize on a person's style than to fight it.

"I quickly recognize how each person prefers to work," he says. "You can tell during the interview. I watch how they fill out the application and how they respond to questions."

Joe takes time at the beginning to observe how new employees respond to information—how they act on it and work with it. Then he assigns tasks according to styles.

"If I want something done fast, I call on Maxine or Ron. Both move like lightning, overcome problems and deliver results quickly."

People like Ralph or Trudy who like to work on details, get a chance to do just that. The talkative, outgoing ones such as Sue and Rob are trained to handle special problems like customer service and new product sales. Those like Dan and Rick who are better at projects than dealing with people are put to work organizing new systems and streamlining procedures.

By staying aware that everyone has some of all styles, Joe works to balance each person's style with new challenges. His people appreciate his sensitivity to their uniqueness.

The next letter in "LEARN" is "R" for "Respect them as Professionals."

As you begin to appreciate the value of the individual to the success of the organization, you create a more respectful environment. Upgrading the workplace with fresh paint, more light and artwork is always a good idea.

But attractive surroundings are not the most important means of showing respect. More important are the ways in which employees are treated in the daily duties of their work.

People instinctively know when they are treated with respect and when they are not. Respecting your employees is a value that needs to be addressed with every meeting, with every act you make as a manager.

Step 4 will give you an opportunity to analyze how well you offer respect to your fellow workers.

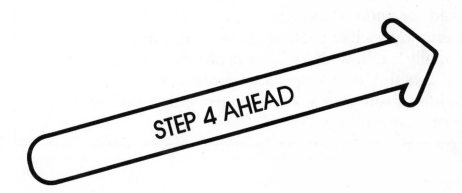

STEP 4 AHEAD

STEP 4: RESPECT EMPLOYEES AS PROFESSIONALS

Two of the most important acts a manager or leader must do is to *treat people with respect and offer recognition when earned.* You know from your own feelings how important these two qualities are in making people happy on the job.

No matter what else is going on, if workers do not get *respect* and *recognition*, they will be eventually unhappy and unproductive.

It's not enough:

- ☑ **to be an efficient manager**
- ☑ **to teach others to think for themselves**
- ☑ **to show employees the end result of their work**
- ☑ **to provide interesting work**
- ☑ **to listen**

or ☑ **to inform**

Employees must also feel respected as a person and recognized for good work. Respect can best be done by treating employees like professionals. Hire them professionally*, talk with them as professionals, and when the going gets tough, ask opinions professionally. When you provide a professional atmosphere, employees will feel and respond accordingly.

For more information on interviewing, order QUALITY INVERVIEWING from the back of the book.

RESPECT EMPLOYEES' FEELINGS

Respect and recognition communicate the worth of an individual. When you communicate respectfully, you are saying, "your feelings are important to me."

Respect is free. It needs to be consistent. You've created a position that requires someone to give an honest day's work in return for your honest day's pay. When you put a person in that position, it is essential that you respect that person's ability to do the job.

You can show respect—or the lack of it—in a number of ways. Check yourself on the following: Give yourself a score of 3 for always, a 2 for some of the time, a 1 for occasionally, a 0 for never.

_____ I greet each person pleasantly each day.

_____ I take time to MBWA (manage by walking around), ask questions, chat and listen.

_____ When I talk with employees, I make eye contact and speak respectfully and pleasantly.

_____ I include them in as many decisions as possible.

_____ I ask for their advice on matters concerning their job, work area or other related items.

_____ I treat everyone equally.

_____ I do not withhold information from any team member.

_____ I call employees by their preferred name.

_____ I do not assign an overload without including essential employees in the decision making process.

_____ I emphasize team spirit.

_____ I do not assign special projects without carefully analyzing the growth needs of my people.

_____ I praise in person when a job is well done.

_____ I correct in private on a job not well done.

_____ I offer coaching to improve job performance and new skills.

_____ I insist on high standards and communicate that respectfully.

_____ SCORE

If you scored 37-45, your folks feel highly respected, 30-36, your folks feel OK, 22-29 they feel you don't respect them very much, 15-21 a revolt is brewing.

RECOGNIZE QUALITY PERFORMANCE

We all love positive recognition—that wonderful moment when someone important lets us know how great we've been.

When we know we've worked hard and earned that moment, *we want it!* Without it, we feel shortchanged, unrewarded, and unvalued. Our spirit falls, the energy goes out of us, our pace slows.

Never underestimate the power of recognition as a motivator. It's the oil that keeps the machinery turning. Studies show that people work harder for recognition than for money.

That's why recognition needs to come both formally and informally. It must also meet these important points:

1. Recognition must be given in a way that treats every person and effort with equal opportunity.

2. It must reward for true accomplishment, not superficial or momentary gain.

3. It must fulfill the goals of the organization, the customer and the employee.

4. It must guide and encourage the worker.

5. It must be done in a positive and public way that encourages others to strive for the same.

6. It must be done informally as well as during a formal time of recognition.

7. Other: _____

_____

_____

_____

A TIME FOR YOU!

In case you feel recognition is flowing more from you to other people and not enough to you, take a moment to recognize your good work. List below some of your best efforts in the past week, month and year. Add any personal acts that made other people feel good about themselves. Include off-the-job deeds, too.

This week I'm proud I did:

_____

_____

_____

_____

Within the last month I'm proud about:

_____

_____

_____

_____

Within the last year I'm proud I was able to accomplish:

_____

_____

_____

_____

Hurray for me!!!!!

BONUS SECTION: *The Power of* 4

Part of getting and giving an honest day's work is realizing how important people are to the success of any organization. As we realize this, we change from thinking of them as tools and concentrate on growing them as resources.

Growing people is like planting a garden. To produce a good crop you start with healthy plants, provide the best start possible and care for them carefully. If you would tend your people as carefully as you would tend a garden that was your only source of food, what kind of crop would you get?

Organizations are not about just making money. They are about growing the business, growing profits (or reaching the goal) and growing people at the same time.

You need four elements to grow good people. Together they are called *THE POWER OF 4*.

For an excellent book on getting employees off to a good start, order NEW EMPLOYEE ORIENTATION from page 73.

SYNCHRONIZED ENERGY

The power of the four elements shown below produces enormous energy. The total power is truly greater than the sum of the parts. Create these four elements and learn to harness them for a powerful workforce.

The Power of 4

VISION	CHALLENGE SKILL DEVELOPMENT
A SENSE OF BELONGING	FUN

These four parts of an effective workplace add up to a whole that is greater than the sum of its parts. These four factors create **synergy.**

Synergy = synchronized energy.

This closes the Commitment Gap!

(Adapted from Warren Bennis and Burt Nanus, *LEADERS:* STRATEGIES FOR TAKING CHARGE, Harper & Row, 1985, p. 82-83.)

THE FUN FACTOR!

The single element getting the most attention from *THE POWER OF* [4] these days is *THE FUN FACTOR*. Enlightened leaders are beginning to realize that fun and work go together. It is an excellent way to develop self-esteem, skill development and a sense of belonging.

The great ''people motivators'' have fun with their team. They have it both while working hard and sometimes by playing hard. They use fun as grease to turn the wheels a little faster while the machinery is running hard and to lubricate it while it is resting.

Research has shown the healing power of laughter when people are ill. Research is also showing the motivating power of fun while working hard. You want an honest day's work? Have some fun!

Fun doesn't have to be costly in time and money. It can be part of the job. It can be as simple as an attitude. Fun usually falls into the following categories: 1) The fun of new skills, 2) the challenge of being the best, 3) taking time off for fun on the premises, or 4) having fun together off site.

CASE
SITUATION #4

As a business owner, Joanne has always been a hard worker. She has owned a beauty salon for 15 years and has 12 people working for her. She has fun with her employees, yet works at being the best salon in the area. Her idea of fun is to be first with new styles and techniques. She rewards hardworking employees with paid trips to shows in Florida or Las Vegas where they learn the latest news in the hairstyling world. Do they socialize after work? You bet, including a picnic in the summer and an end-of-year party. The rest of the time they have fun at being the best.

Patrick is a manager for a large computer company. He has a sales force of 25 people and spends time with each one. He gives lots of ''strokes'' for good work. Patrick notices little things his team does well and comments accordingly. He is high on recognition and the sales forces seems to thrive on it. After exceeding major sales goals, Patrick arranges fun events such as theme parties or scavenger hunts. Whatever it takes for a feeling of belonging to something special is something Patrick is willing to do. It is no wonder he has been consistently recognized for superior sales performance over the years.

The next letter in "LEARN" is "N" which stands for "Never Stifle Personal Growth."

The last step on your climb to motivating your people to give their best is to create opportunities for personal growth. Without that the lid is on tight. People stagnate and languish. When you have provided the other four levels of employee need, keep on going.

The great payoff for encouraging growth among your employees is that you as manager will inevitably grow. If you spend your energies controlling people and keeping them from growing, you have no energy left to grow. On the other hand, when you create growth for others, you create it for yourself.

Step 5 gives you the opportunity to measure your IQ—your Innovation Quotient. Like all the other self-assessment quizzes in this book, this one is designed to provide you with guidelines for new management techniques.

Congratulations on a successful climb. After you finish Step 5, create a celebration for yourself and your staff!

STEP 5: NEVER STIFLE PERSONAL GROWTH

The last step to successful people management is to *give employees room to grow*. The greatest satisfaction workers will have in the future will be to be challenged in their work and grow in new skill development.

The world is changing faster and faster. An employee's only hope to keep up with it is to grow in understanding and skill development. Your job as a leader is to provide that opportunity.

If you remember, *interesting work* was one of the first points covered in this book. Even if work is interesting, it remains that way only to a point. It is then your job to provide more challenge and skill development.

There may be a high level of challenge and skill development in your work currently. If so, congratulations! However, remember that all levels need to be satisfied for people to be happy.

It's up to you, the leader, to create an atmosphere of innovation. This means you open your own mind to new and better ways of doing things and then open your workers' minds to the same.

HOW HIGH IS YOUR I.Q.?

How do you create a spirit of innovation? Check your I.Q.—your *Innovation Quotient*. There are people who criticize what's wrong, people who suggest better ways for other people to do things and people who find a better way to do them. Which category are you in?

Take this quick self-test to check your Innovation Quotient. Score 3 for always, 2 for sometimes, 1 for once in a while, 0 for never.

_____ 1. Are you a sleuth? Do you look under the surface of what's going on—problems, trends, feedback from others?

_____ 2. Are you an "innovation opportunist?" Do you find opportunities for solving problems, creating wants, filling needs?

_____ 3. Are you a strategist? Do you spend time redefining your goals, correcting your course and revising plans to reach them?

_____ 4. Are you a challenger? Do you examine assumptions, biases, preconceived beliefs for loopholes and opportunities?

_____ 5. Are you a trend spotter? Do you actively monitor change in your field such as technology, politics, or attitudes to spot opportunity early?

_____ 6. Are you a connector? Do you keep your eye peeled for concepts you can borrow from one field and apply to another?

_____ 7. Are you a risk taker? Are you willing to develop and experiment with ideas of your own?

_____ 8. How's your intuition? Do you rely on your true feelings?

_____ 9. Are you a simplifier? Can you reduce complex decisions to a few simple questions by seeing the "big picture?"

_____ 10. Are you a need filler? Do you look for the human need behind statistics?

_____ 11. Are you a visionary? Do you think farther ahead than most of your colleagues? Do you think long term? Describe your vision to others?

_____ 12. Are you resourceful? Do you dig up research and information to argue your side? Do you use information creatively?

_____ 13. Are you a listener and feedback junkie? Do you look forward to hearing from others about your blind spots? Do you welcome ''better ideas'' from others?

_____ 14. Are you an innovation networker? Do you have numbers of contacts with whom you communicate to share thinking, get excited about a new approach or idea? Do you seek out other innovative thinkers?

_____ 15. Are you a futurist? Do you hang out at ''The Cutting Edge'' saloon with other crystal ball watchers? Are you fascinated by the future?

_____ 16. Are you a reader? Do you devour books, magazines, articles that deal with success stories, innovation in general, in your field of interest in particular?

_____ Score

A score of 41-48 shows you paused just long enough in your pursuit of a vision to answer these questions. We'll see your name in lights some day. 36-40 shows you're ready to step up to team playing with the ''discoverers.'' 30-36 you're awake and willing and a good support person. Below 29 You're a maintainer and conservator of the past. Your talents seem to lie in other areas.

WHAT IS YOUR ORGANIZATION'S I.Q.?

An innovative organization breeds innovative people. Take a look at your work atmosphere:

_____ 1. Is innovation highly regarded in your organization?

_____ 2. Is innovation built into the strategy of your organization?

_____ 3. Is innovation implemented quickly?

_____ 4. Does your organization have a "skunk works?"*

_____ 5. Do you have a meeting to discuss opportunities as often as you have one to discuss problems?

_____ 6. Are your reporting systems set up for qualitative as well as quantitative information?

_____ 7. Do you staff innovative processes with your best and brightest?

_____ 8. Do you always keep before you the purpose of your product or service?

_____ 9. Do you celebrate innovation with ceremony?

_____ 10. Are innovators treated like heroes?

_____ Score

A score of 24-30 indicates an organization which highly values and rewards innovation. 17-23 deserves a "well done!" You're alive, awake, and enthusiastic about developing your people. 10-16, rev up your motors to catch up! Below 10, arthritis is setting in. You're moving too slowly to keep up in the market and keep good people.

(*"Skunk works" is a term made popular in the best-selling *IN SEARCH OF EXCELLENCE* by Tom Peters and Robert Waterman. It is used to describe a hideout workplace, a "boiler room" where workers get together after hours to work on a challenging project such as the first micro-computer.)

HOW DO YOU DO IT?

How do you foster innovation in your organization? You need to develop a positive attitude,* a commitment and some ground rules.

ATTITUDE

- You need an attitude that encourages openness, curiosity, willingness to experiment.

COMMITMENT

- You need to commit to innovation as a value in the vision of your organization.

GROUND RULES

You need to develop the following:
- Be flexible
- Be open about feelings
- Be fair
- Have fun
- Be detached—some ideas don't work
- Be encouraging

---

*Read ATTITUDE: YOUR MOST PRICELESS POSSESSION (See the back of the book).

HOW DOES YOUR GARDEN GROW?

If you are innovative but your organization is not, how do you encourage your people to bring out their innovative tendencies? Give yourself a 3 for Yes!, 2 for sometimes, 1 for occasionally, 0 for never.

_____ I help them set goals for new skill development.

_____ I celebrate any progress with them.

_____ I reinforce points along the way.

_____ I send them out of the office for growth experiences.

_____ I keep them posted on new developments in their field.

_____ I encourage them to read and take courses.

_____ I create time for my personal skill development.

_____ I create challenges for them.

_____ I value their input.

_____ I spend time discussing opportunities with them.

_____ I foster a ''skunk works'' time and place.

_____ I recognize innovative performance.

_____ Other _____

_____ Score

29-36 You're a leader as mountain climber. 23-28 You're a great burden bearer on the trek. 15-22 You'll do as base camp support. Below 14—you missed the boat. You are a couch potato.

Bonus Section: *Your Score Sheet*

Take a moment to record your scores from the previous self-assessment pages in this workbook:

1. Are you Giving the Top Ten? (p. 15)   SCORE _____

2. The Efficient Manager's Checklist (p. 20)   SCORE _____

3. Make Work Interesting (p. 30)   SCORE _____

4. Your Listening and Informing Survey (p. 38)   SCORE _____

5. Respect Their Feelings (p. 49)   SCORE _____

6. Your Innovation Quotient (p. 59)   SCORE _____

7. What is Your Organization's I.Q.? (p. 60)   SCORE _____

8. How Does Your Garden Grow? (p. 62)   SCORE _____

Your Total SCORE: _____

Of the possible 312 points, if you scored over 250 consider yourself a superior leader. Over 200 a very good leader. Over 150 on the right track but need help. Under 150, more training is needed to make you an effective leader.

Now that you've completed the five steps of getting an honest day's work, it's time to set some goals.

As you know, goals are meant to help you get where you want to go. Set some goals now to help you attain the five levels of employee satisfaction.

GOAL SETTING...START HERE!

Begin your development plan by analyzing what level of need each employee needs most. Check off the satisfaction levels of each of your staff. Leave blank those qualities you think need attention. A 1 is survival, 2 is security, 3 is a need to belong, 4 is prestige and 5 is a need for self-fulfillment:

NAME	1	2	3	4	5

With each employee begin to supply the lowest level of need first. If Joe is missing both survival and self-fulfillment needs, survival will be more important. Prepare a plan for filling that need. Include a calendar on which you mark off time to prepare a plan, create conference time with each person and follow through as needed.

YOUR DEVELOPMENT PLAN

Go back to page 15 and record your score for each element. Color in from left to right how far you are in each one. For instance, if you gave yourself a 3 on efficiency, color all the way across. If you gave yourself a 1 or 0, color in appropriately.

	0	1	2	3
1. I am an efficient manager.				
2. I encourage them to think.				
3. I show the end results of work.				
4. I offer interesting work.				
5. I listen to employees.				
6. I keep them informed.				
7. I treat them with respect.				
8. I recognize and praise good work.				
9. I offer challenge.				
10. I encourage skill development.				

Now you know where to begin to increase your effectiveness as a manager and leader. On the next two pages outline your plan for improving your performance and reaching some of your own goals.

AIM FOR THE TOP

1st goal	2nd goal	3rd goal	4th goal

Step 1: What Do I Want To Accomplish?

Step 2: What Is Keeping Me From It?

Step 3: What KSAs (knowledge, skills and abilities) Do I Need?

Step 4: Whose Help Do I Need?

Step 5: What's In It For Me?

CONTINUE YOUR CLIMB

1st goal	2nd goal	3rd goal	4th goal

Step 6: What Sign Will I Look For That I'm Reaching It?

Step 7: What Are The First Steps I Need To Take?

Step 8: What Comes After That?

Step 9: What Do I Do If Things Go Wrong?

Step 10: What's The Earliest/Latest Possible Completion Date?

CASE SITUATION #5

It's not easy to provide challenge and skill development unless it's written into your plan. Time slips by and systems work well enough that new skills sometimes seem a luxury a leader can't afford.

Diane, a head nurse in a drug and alcohol rehabilitation unit at a major metropolitan hospital, creates time for her people to sharpen their skills.

No matter how heavy the load, she insists her nurses take the necessary time to review cases for their new patients. That way they can be completely prepared and professional during the first meeting. She also sets aside lunch on a bi-weekly basis to discuss news in the field and encourage ideas on how to do things better.

Diane makes sure her staff attends seminars that motivate as well as educate them. She sees her staff as a close support system for each other, as well as for the patients. Their spirits need constant refreshing because of the intensive nature of the work. "I know how important the stimulation of new skills is as well as the need for quiet time for planning and preparation. A constant demand on energy and skills without replenishment is no fun and eventually destroys effectiveness," she says.

SECTION III

PRACTICE WHAT YOU'VE LEARNED

TOUCH THEIR HEARTS

Each level of employee satisfaction and each quality therein touches the nerve ending of a vital need. Remember that as you go about your work as leader and manager.

Every manager touches the needs of each employee every day. As a manager you can ignore these needs, manipulate them for your own ends, or fulfill them for the satisfaction of all—including customers and others in your organization.

Choose to fulfill your employees' needs. Your life will be richer and freer. Your own climb will be that much higher as you bring out the potential within your people. Give them what they want, and they'll give you what you want.

Touch their hearts and they'll give you theirs. Aim for the heart.

TWO-WEEK CHECKLIST

Date ___/___/___

It's easy to read and file this book. You may nod knowingly as you look over the pages and think, "I knew that." But unless you make a commitment to follow through, you will not have closed your own Commitment Gap to better leadership.

To avoid losing the impact of the points covered in these pages, get started today. Two weeks after reading this workbook, check your progress by completing the following exercise:

_____ I have started to increase my leadership skills.

_____ I have filled out my "Aim For The Top" goal sheet.

_____ I have incorporated those goals into a daily and weekly plan.

_____ I have programmed time for each employee on an informal basis.

_____ I have listed the needs of each employee and begun to work on a plan.

_____ Each plan is incorporated into my calendar so that I make sure I do what I committed to do.

_____ I have concrete goals so that I know when I'm making progress.

_____ I give myself respect and recognition when I complete each new task.

_____ I'm on my way to being a "superior leader."

THREE-WEEK CHECKLIST

Date   /   /

_____ I can now give the top ten qualities (page 16) to my employees and get an average score of 25 or better.

_____ I have incorporated all 10 points into a standard operating procedure.

_____ I am on my way to liberating the potential of my people!

_____ I also notice a difference in my own performance.

_____ I aim for the top when I work with people, not just my staff, but everyone.

ONE-MONTH CHECKLIST

Date __/__/__

_____ I have tracked the three reasons the job doesn't get done.

_____ I have rearranged the work flow as needed.

_____ I have shown my employees the end result of their work.

_____ I have varied the pace and variety of their work for interest.

_____ I am sensitive to respecting their needs.

_____ I have begun to encourage people to think for themselves.

_____ I offer recognition by _____

_____

_____ I've created a "skunk works" for greater creativity.

DON'T STOP NOW! KEEP THAT PROGRESS GOING!

ABOUT THE FIFTY-MINUTE SERIES

"Fifty-Minute books are the best new publishing idea in years. They are clear, practical, concise and affordable — perfect for today's world."

Leo Hauser
(Past President, ASTD)

What Is A Fifty-Minute Book?

—Fifty-Minute books are brief, soft-cover, "self-study" modules which cover a single concept. They are reasonably priced, and ideal for formal training programs, excellent for self-study and perfect for remote location training.

Why Are Fifty-Minute Books Unique?

—Because of their format and level. Designed to be "read with a pencil," the basics of a subject can be quickly grasped and applied through a series of hands-on activities, exercises and cases.

How Many Fifty-Minute Books Are There?

—Those listed on the facing page at this time, however, additional titles are in development. For more information write to **Crisp Publications, Inc., 95 First Street, Los Altos, CA 94022.**

Crisp books are distributed in Canada by Reid Publishing, Ltd., P.O. Box 7267, Oakville, Ontario, Canada L6J 6L6.

In Australia by Career Builders, P.O. Box 1051 Springwood, Brisbane, Queensland, Australia 4127.

And in New Zealand by Career Builders, P.O. Box 571, Manurewa, New Zealand.

THE FIFTY-MINUTE SERIES

Quantity	Title	Code #	Price	Amount
	The Fifty-Minute Supervisor—*2nd Edition*	58-0	$6.95	
	Effective Performance Appraisals—*Revised*	11-4	$6.95	
	Successful Negotiation—*Revised*	09-2	$6.95	
	Quality Interviewing—*Revised*	13-0	$6.95	
	Team Building: An Exercise in Leadership—*Revised*	16-5	$7.95	
	Performance Contracts: The Key To Job Success—*Revised*	12-2	$6.95	
	Personal Time Management	22-X	$6.95	
	Effective Presentation Skills	24-6	$6.95	
	Better Business Writing	25-4	$6.95	
	Quality Customer Service	17-3	$6.95	
	Telephone Courtesy & Customer Service	18-1	$6.95	
	Restaurant Server's Guide To Quality Service—*Revised*	08-4	$6.95	
	Sales Training Basics—*Revised*	02-5	$6.95	
	Personal Counseling—*Revised*	14-9	$6.95	
	Balancing Home & Career	10-6	$6.95	
	Mental Fitness: A Guide To Emotional Health	15-7	$6.95	
	Attitude: Your Most Priceless Possession	21-1	$6.95	
	Preventing Job Burnout	23-8	$6.95	
	Successful Self-Management	26-2	$6.95	
	Personal Financial Fitness	20-3	$7.95	
	Job Performance and Chemical Dependency	27-0	$7.95	
	Career Discovery—*Revised*	07-6	$6.95	
	Study Skills Strategies—*Revised*	05-X	$6.95	
	I Got The Job!—*Revised*	59-9	$6.95	
	Effective Meetings Skills	33-5	$7.95	
	The Business of Listening	34-3	$6.95	
	Professional Sales Training	42-4	$7.95	
	Customer Satisfaction: The Other Half of Your Job	57-2	$7.95	
	Managing Disagreement Constructively	41-6	$7.95	
	Professional Excellence for Secretaries	52-1	$6.95	
	Starting A Small Business: A Resource Guide	44-0	$7.95	
	Developing Positive Assertiveness	38-6	$6.95	
	Writing Fitness-Practical Exercises for Better Business Writing	35-1	$7.95	
	An Honest Day's Work: Motivating Employees to Give Their Best	39-4	$6.95	
	Marketing Your Consulting & Professional Services	40-8	$7.95	
	Time Management On The Telephone	53-X	$6.95	
	Training Managers to Train	43-2	$7.95	
	New Employee Orientation	46-7	$6.95	
	The Art of Communicating: Achieving Impact in Business	45-9	$7.95	
	Technical Presentation Skills	55-6	$7.95	
	Plan B: Protecting Your Career from the Winds of Change	48-3	$7.95	
	A Guide To Affirmative Action	54-8	$7.95	
	Memory Skills in Business	56-4	$6.95	

(Continued on next page)

THE FIFTY-MINUTE SERIES
(Continued)

☐ Send volume discount information.

☐ Add my name to CPI's mailing list.

	Amount
Total (from other side)	
Shipping ($1.50 first book, $.50 per title thereafter)	
California Residents add 7% tax	
Total	

Ship to: _____

_____

_____

_____

Phone number: _____

Bill to: _____

_____

_____

P.O. # _____

**All orders except those with a P.O.# must be prepaid.
Call (415) 949-4888 for more information.**

BUSINESS REPLY
FIRST CLASS   PERMIT NO. 884   LOS ALTOS, CA

POSTAGE WILL BE PAID BY ADDRESSEE

Crisp Publications, Inc.
95 First Street
Los Altos, CA 94022

NOTES

NOTES